THE

the *ROAD* TO
HAPPINESS

WORDS OF WISDOM FROM THE
WORLD'S HAPPIEST NATION

GYONPO TSHERING

EDITED BY MARGARET GEE

SKYHORSE
PUBLISHING

Skyhorse Publishing books may be purchased in bulk at special discounts for sales promotion, corporate gifts, fund-raising, or educational purposes. Special editions can also be created to specifications. For details, contact the Special Sales Department, Skyhorse Publishing, 307 West 36th Street, 11th Floor, New York, NY 10018 or info@skyhorsepublishing.com.

Skyhorse® and Skyhorse Publishing® are registered trademarks of Skyhorse Publishing, Inc.®, a Delaware corporation.
Visit our website at www.skyhorsepublishing.com.

10 9 8 7 6 5 4 3 2 1

Library of Congress Cataloging-in-Publication Data is available on file.

ISBN: 978-1-61608-872-9

Printed in China

The Road to Happiness is dedicated

to

the 4th coronation anniversary of His Majesty
the King Jigme Khesar Namgyel Wangchuck, for
bringing unprecedented economic prosperity, social
harmony, and happiness under his glorious reign.

INTRODUCTION

Bhutan is flanked by India, China and Tibet—a tiny jewel of a country nestled in the Eastern Himalayas between two immense superpowers. This position may make it seem vulnerable, but its values—a devotion to the highest principles of human existence—give it strength.

Bhutan is the first and only country in the world to have a government edict that Gross National Happiness (GNH) is more important than Gross National Product. The principal of GNH (emphasizing a selfless service to others and the search for enlightenment) is a core value of this unique Buddhist kingdom. They have a designated Gross National Happiness Center which is a magnet for scholars and experts studying this innovative philosophy, which will spread this message to a wider, troubled world.

The concept of GNH has received international media coverage and "happiness" conferences seem to be springing up worldwide like the vibrant crimson and pink rhododendrons that cascade down the hillsides in the Bhutanese spring. The current Prime Minister of Bhutan, Jingme Y. Thinley, recently addressed the United Nations in New York on the concept of Gross National Happiness.

Bhutan has a lot it can teach us.

Bhutan is entirely original. It appears on first visit to be a simple country with a village-based subsistence lifestyle. Yet beneath the surface, it is a rich, diverse community ranging from yak herders and the nomadic Laya people to a complex royal and government hierarchy, overseen by scholars, gurus, rimpoches, high lamas, abbots, senior monks, and some of the most environmentally devout practitioners in the world. (Bhutan is the only country in the world to have banned cigarette smoking and was the first to ban plastic bags in 1999.)

The landscape is dotted with buildings decorated with flowers and Buddhist art called dzongs, chortens, and innumerable monasteries. The most famous of these is the stunning Tiger's Nest or Taktshang monastery which clings to the steep hillsides in the Upper Paro Valley surrounded by blue pine and spruce forests. The revered Guru Padmasambhava who is credited with introducing Buddhism to Bhutan, is said to have meditated here for three months in the 8th Century.

Even if you have a very secular or agnostic view of religion, it is hard not to be moved by the intense and highly visible Buddhist practices, ceremonies, monuments, stories, festivals, fables, chants, incantations and offerings to their gods, goddesses, and other deities which are an everyday part of Bhutanese life.

Ultimately, it is the Bhutanese themselves who are so engaging, and they really do seem to live the way of loving kindness and compassion—the major tenets of the Mahayana Buddhism to which they subscribe. They should also be much better known for their great capacity for jokes and laughter. They seem to live in the moment, and have as their highest priorities community, family, and faith.

From the time I arrive there until I leave, I just feel happier in Bhutan than anywhere else on the planet, and can't seem to wipe the smile off my face!

Perhaps it will be the wisdom from one of the smallest and happiest nations on earth, Bhutan, which will ultimately provide the necessary guidance for stability and peace so longed for throughout the world, when so many nations appear to be afflicted and deeply disturbed by war, poverty, and palpable misery. But, like every great journey, the first step begins with us.

Gyonpo Tshering and I sincerely hope that *The Road to Happiness* will illuminate your own path to enhanced happiness, tranquility and well-being.

Tashi Delek. Margaret Gee, April 2012

FOREWORD

This collection of original proverbs by Gyonpo Tshering perfectly captures the essence of Bhutan's unique policy of Gross National Happiness. The intriguing aspect of these wise, witty and enlightening proverbs is that these remarkable sayings have come from deep within Bhutan. They truly reflect the Bhutanese people's dedication to following the Buddha's path and treating others with respect, kindness, and compassion. And, last but not least they embody the nation's wonderful sense of humor!

The Road to Happiness is an ideal companion for either ordinary folks or scholars who are seeking to discover the true nature of Bhutan's philosophy and Government edict that Gross National Happiness is more important than Gross National Product. These beautiful and endearing proverbs are truly a mirror to the heart and soul of the proud and innovative Bhutanese people. Our message to the world is very simple: be kind, compassionate, and affectionate and see the bigger picture. Be connected to your faith, your family and your community. And enjoy life too!

This engaging collection of proverbs researched and collected by the renowned Bhutanese scholar Gyonpo

Tshering is a treasure trove of wise counsel, enlightening reflections, and some funny sayings too.

It will put a smile on your face, and deepen your knowledge and understanding about the unique and caring nature of our compassionate monarch of the Bhutanese people in our beautiful little Eastern Himalayan Kingdom.

His Excellency Lyonpo Minjur Dorji
Honourable Minister for Home and Cultural Affairs
Royal Government of Bhutan

Human life is like a butter lamp
flickering in the wind.

✧

Proverbs are a garland of precious ancient
jewels to wear around the mind and heart.

Like there is no beam without
a supporting pillar.
There can be no education without a
strong teacher.

✧

The seedlings of spiritual devotion are
hit hard by the hailstorm of laziness.

If you search for happiness you will
not find it. If happiness searches for
you it will always find you.

❖

The sunshine of a Lama's mandala
is necessary to remove the darkness
of spiritual unawareness.

A flea springs up from a cozy blanket
A hero springs up from a rocky ledge.

✧

A yak herder takes the credit but it is the
poor yak which carries the heavy load.

Cold weather doesn't care if
your coat is old or new.

❖

The milk of the snow leopard is nectar
from the gods of the Himalayas.

A king can only do so much to protect
a lawbreaker, as a Lama can only do
so much to protect a sinner.

·⟡·

The doctor's son can get ill and even
the astrologer's horse can get lost.

When you have climbed hard to the mountain pass you will be rewarded with the sight of a flowery meadow.

❖

If the company you keep encourages you to steal, your moral compass has already been stolen.

Without a blessed life, even gold
or silver have no value.

❖

A person who cannot keep their promises
is like a tree with a rotting trunk.

Even a howling snowstorm will not
silence the melody of a lark's voice.

✧

Singing a song with a clear and
open mind is better than reciting
a mantra with a bad attitude.

Even if a cup breaks don't forget
the beautiful picture on it.

✣

If you don't truly understand the true meaning
of the Buddha's sutras and tantras you will
just be reciting the texts like a parrot.

Pile up good deeds in this life and in the next
life you will have mountains of happiness.

✧

If you say nasty things about people sooner or
later you will meet your victim face to face.

When a fool makes a mistake the pond
ripples.
When a learned scholar makes a mistake
there can be a tidal wave.

✦

A white lion can be famous, but only a
loyal guard dog can protect your house.

If you have not experienced great suffering
and great happiness you will find
it hard to tell them apart.

Suffering always ends, and so does happiness.

Do not chirrup too much about your happiness and do not whine too much about your unhappiness.

✧

Parents are like walnuts, hard on the outside and soft on the inside.

Happiness and suffering are like the
Summer sun.
One moment it is shining and the next
it is covered by dark clouds.

❖

There is one moment of human birth,
but a hundred ways to die.

Growing old physically is not
true old age.
That only comes with growing
old mentally.

❖

People who are not careful what they say tend
not to be careful with the rest of their body.

The wind never stops blowing
and the river never rests.

✧

Profits in your hand can mean a loss
will soon be dropped at your feet.

A rich heart is better than money in the bank.

✧

It is better to die among the prudent
and conscientious than among
the reckless and shameless.

An elephant wishes he could jump
like a flea, and a flea wishes he could
be strong like an elephant.

❖

It is better to be a wise owl
than a cunning monkey.

A rope can bind just one, but a
harsh law can bind millions.

✧

Anger is a golden opportunity
to practise patience.

If a female dog does not wag its tail, a male dog will not perk up his ears.

✧

The sun is the greatest jewel of all.

The frog in the pond is doomed if he only
dreams of swimming in the ocean.

❖

A man or woman without a good legacy
is like a horse which has become lame.

If you fly on the wings of a drunken eagle
you will very soon fall to the ground.

⟡

In the bed of a high achiever you will
find the corpse of an ordinary person.

If you quarrel the gods will trouble you.
If you are friendly the demons
will leave you alone.

✤

If you find someone who loves you
as much as your parents you are
sure to have a happy family.

We are all shepherds, so learn how
to tend kindly to your flock.

Angrily rebuking a quiet and thoughtful person
is like trampling on the petals of a rose.

The leaves rustling in a gentle breeze is the same sound as the voice of a goddess.

✧

Tigers have stripes on the outside, people have stripes within.

If you are happy in your home even when
you are away you will never feel homesick.

✧

When people tell lies their
souls begin to crumble.

It is better to plant flowers than
to build monuments.

✧

When a bad thing happens you feel like
a rock plummeting down a crevasse.

Even if the tap runs dry you can always count on it raining again soon.

✧

If two old friends reconcile it should be like two rivers meeting, a waterfall of affection and happiness.

Speaking out of turn is like
wearing ill-fitting clothes.

✧

A good king can take you to the top
of the mountain but a bad one
will push you over the edge.

Make sure you can tell the difference between
the prints of a tiger and a domestic cat.

❖

If your leader turns into a dog be sure
to ask why he is wagging his tail.

You cannot broaden your horizons by staying at home, or spare the oceans without saving water.

⚜

Even though an ant appears to be small
and weak it has the strength and
determination of a buffalo.

Just as the peacock can change its colours
a monk can transform offerings.

Ф

During bad times good friends are essential.
During good times bad friends
are still unnecessary.

Do not expect a donkey to be able to
carry the same load as an elephant.

✧

You can create your own happiness
or your own misery.

Even the sun can be eclipsed so be
aware of your own limitations.

✧

A man who wears a dog mask will not roar
like a lion.
A man wearing a lion mask will not bark
like a dog.

The wisdom of our ancestors will be there
for as long as a crow's feathers are black.

⋄

People who go on acquiring things they don't
need can eventually lose everyone they value.

Negative thoughts can so easily slip into
negative and destructive actions.

✧

Even while it sleeps the cat
dreams of the mouse.

A fool rushes across a field of snow but a
wise person first makes sure there
are no holes to fall into.

✲

You don't need sunshine to warm
your good fortune.
It should by itself warm your
heart and soul.

If you don't communicate well you will disturb
the minds of others. If you don't know how
to listen you will disturb your own mind.

✧

If you take an oath lightly one day
it could weigh you down.

Don't become obsessed with making a
mountain of money, otherwise you
will fall into an abyss of despair.

✧

What we have already achieved is the size
of a fingernail, what is left for others to
do is your height from head to toe.

The temple may be ancient but the
meaning is always modern.

❖

A demon you know is better
than an unknown deity.

A human being abandoned by a Lama
feels like a tree that has been uprooted.

❖

Saying nasty things about other people
is as odious as smelly shoes.

Don't cross a swiftly flowing river unless
you want to end up drifting
helplessly in the ocean.

❖

You should protect your possessions, but if
something is stolen perhaps someone
needed the object more than you.

Real intelligence is not about what you say
but how you behave towards others.

✧

One dream cannot rest on two pillows.

Evil words are like poisonous flowers
Evil actions are like poisonous roots.

❖

It is more important to have good teeth in your
head than a hat which fits properly on it.

You cannot be gentle like a beautiful tree
if your tongue cuts others like an axe.

❖

Kind words sow the seeds of the lotus.
Cruel words sow the seeds of poison ivy.

If you take a wrong path you can turn around
but harsh words can never be taken back.

❖

A dragon's roar is soon forgotten but
a rainbow's beauty lasts forever.

It is better to cherish a swiftly flowing river
than to run off at the mouth like a drain.

❖

When arguments are settled with money
everyone is impoverished.

If disputes are not peacefully resolved
the volcano will continue to erupt.

✧

If you don't repay your debts you
will be repaid with bad karma.

A bribe is like a moustache, it covers
the truth beneath the skin.

✧

Truth is medicine.
Lying is poison.

Empty words are like empty plates.
They make people hungry for
genuine nourishment.

❖

Sweets are delicious to eat as proverbs
are delectable to hear.

Your health will be better if you receive
a blessing from a Lama.

❖

If your aspirations are unrealistically high
you may emotionally spiral out of control.

The wisdom of India, Bhutan and Tibet can
cleanse your soul,
but you have to make the decision to journey
in these spiritual countries.

❖

In the same way that there is gold in the earth,
there is Buddha nature in all sentient beings.

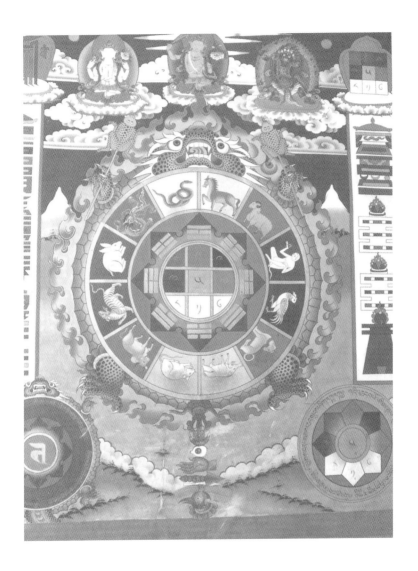

A happy life is like the blink of an eye, but a miserable life is a never-ending journey.

✧

When faced with imminent danger a regal tiger will tremble just as much as a street dog.

People who are mean with money are usually
mean with their love and friendship.

❖

Life is like footprints in the snow.
Every step will show.

If you are always on a fishing expedition
for a better life, the surface of your
spiritual ocean will never be calm.

✧

Your God will always support you,
but ultimately you are on your
own spiritual journey.

No gold in the ground can ever be more
beautiful than a sunbeam.

❖

You can choose not to speak, but it is
impossible to silence idle chatter in the streets.

No trader could ever make money
selling bad behaviour.

✧

If you are honest the birds in the sky
will befriend you.
If you are dishonest your own son or
daughter will avoid you.

Just when you get the hang of being young, old age taps you on the shoulder.

⋄

Happiness comes from
mental freedom.
Suffering comes from an
emotional prison.

If you value your own life, don't take
the life of other sentient creatures.

❖

If you don't think for yourself, your mouth
will broadcast the will of others.

Be calm and dignified if you are ever invited
to the Palace of a powerful king. Therein
lies the way of mutual respect.

∴

When luck favours us the blessings
of the Lamas have borne fruit.

Your children are the fire and
light in your heart.

✧

Your father's work often looks easy as your
mother's delicious cooking can seem easy too.
Both happen because of skill and hard work.

Knowledge is a useful pathway, but experience will get you to the destination faster.

✧

As your age travels to the highest mountain peaks, your backbone bends towards the valley.

If you don't deliver a parcel you are a thief.
If you don't deliver a message
you are also a thief.

❖

Talk without experience and practice
is like a bird with no feathers.

You have to walk the talk otherwise your religious devotion is a stagnant river.

A single terrible lie may cost you a lifelong trust.

It is more important to think well
of your lifetime partner than to feel
affection for a passing stranger.

✧

If you roll in the muck of life you
will never purify your soul.

Your karmic destiny book is already written.

✧

As there is a different language for each valley in Bhutan, there is a different religious practice for each Lama.

When the valleys of the mind are flooded even
the sacred retreat caves will not save you.

Live simply. Leave only footprints and
carry only your shadow. This is the way.

I would rather have a university degree than an ornate piece of jewellery which could be stolen.

❖

When the karmic wind blows, the
karmic rain is not far away.

The body does not want to be polluted
with disease as the mind does not
want to be muddy with sorrow.

❖

If you have a calm mind your body will
be tranquil.
If your body is calm then it will help to
calm your mind.

Quality not quantity is the key to happiness.

A bad harvest can be replanted and yield a good crop. A bad partner is harder to replace.

A lousy harvest lasts a year, but cruel words can resonate for a lifetime.

Even if we are told we only have a few years to live, we still need to employ the wisdom passed down through the ages.

Life is short but education lasts
at least a hundred years.

✧

It is folly to forget that you are merely
human, and to lust after the
wealth of celestial beings.

Telling secrets is like spilling melted butter.

If you hurt someone you love it is like
a fingernail being torn from flesh.

Just the way vegetables taste better with cheese, human beings are happier living as couples than surviving alone.

❖

The eyes of the beloved deceased will still watch you in the afterlife.

Don't tell everybody everything. Have respect for your privacy and innermost thoughts.

Don't make your will as soon as you get sick, it could hasten your passing away.

We all emerge from the Eastern pass at birth
and depart from the Western pass in death.

✧

Be like the sun and always rise, and the
country stream which keeps gently flowing.

If you have no debts you are rich, and if you have no quarrels you are happier.

⁘

When the dawn breaks the world smiles with happiness and joy.

The tree and the mushroom will rot together, and the meadow and the flower will fade together.

What is more beautiful than the sun illuminating a mountain with a pink and orange glow, or a bird singing happily in a tree-top?

If you have something on your mind get it out, just as it is important to remove grubs eating the bark of a tree.

One lie will vanquish a hundred truths.

A muddy sty is a palace to a pig.

Not everything you hear is true, nor all
unpleasant things the enemy of your happiness.

Explanations don't always solve the
mysteries of life as crying does not
always heal the pain of sadness.

❖

Some things are only written on
the paper of the mind.

If there is no inner contentment it doesn't help
even if your path is strewn with diamonds.

✧

If you throw a stone at a bird,
your sky may fall in.

Just as there are green fertile pastures
and barren plains, the same is true for
the territory of the heart and mind.

✦

You can never completely trust the human
mind until true enlightenment is attained.

Be like a wild animal and have an
acute sense of smell for danger.

✧

Even if some people saw a Buddha flying in the
sky they would not have faith in what they have
seen. In the same way some people will not
have compassion even if they see a poor animal
suffering in a field.

Every king has one evil minister just
as each Buddha has a demon.

✧

Practise the dharma for the sake of
enlightenment, as you raise your
children to love and respect you.

It is a bad thing in the court of life if the
verdict is passed before the witness has spoken.

✤

Telling proverbs to old people is as insulting
as teaching the alphabet to the Buddha.

Even though the Buddha has the hook
of genuine guidance people without
faith will not hang their hats on it.

✧

If you find a piece of turquoise at your
doorstep this is a very auspicious omen. If
you find an animal on the high mountain
he may carry you safely down.

A snow leopard reigns supreme in the mountains but is sometimes treated like a stray dog in the village.

✦

We are what we are. A tiger does not try to be a lion and vice-versa.

It is more important to have a beautiful
mind, than a beautiful face.

✧

You don't have to smile if you are pleased,
nor do you have to frown if you are
displeased. People who do this
don't get so many wrinkles!

Thoughts roam around like a galloping
horse, instead of being contained
in the palm of your hand.

❖

A fickle mind, two-faced behaviour, and a lying
nature, these three can
never be friends.

Limiting your eating is good for your
health, and not fighting with your wife
or husband is good for your heart.

⁘

Too much food can be poisonous
to your health, and too much anger
can poison your friendships.

Good spiritual connections lead to Buddhahood, and bad spiritual connections lead to Hell.

If you are given a jug of good quality wine, repay the favour with fresh water from a mountain spring. Both are enriching.

Money doesn't make people happy,
but neither does poverty. Share what
you have for a better world.

᠅

People who roar like tigers at home,
and are sweet as pussycats in public,
will always scratch you.

Eating and loving is natural, but the right
teacher can give you some good tips
for making it a better experience.

✦

If there are too many carpenters the
door may not shut properly.

Evil is the vilest type of hatred, and
patience the most sought after virtue.

*

It's okay to let go of the moon, for the mandala
of the sun will still rise in the morning.

People with good manners argue about seating, people with bad manners argue about what food is being served.

❖

How you behave is the barometer of your good manners.

The voices of your ancestors will echo
in the valley of your heart forever.

✧

We never see where the arrow came
from, only where it lands.

Pray that the wisdom eyes of the
Buddha looks upon you, otherwise
you are at the whim of the world.

❖

The eyes of true wisdom never
stray across the horizon.

Even if you were only in the company of the Buddha you would probably quarrel sometimes.

⁂

Don't throw mud into someone else's unpolluted stream.

Learn how to be happy with a few garments, instead of lusting for a wardrobe full of luxurious clothes. Like the tiger we can only wear one coat at a time.

✧

Sometimes the poorest people are the most generous, and the richest in spirit.

It is better to sit at the feet of the learned,
than to be at the head of a table of idiots.

✢

Only arrogant people think that
arrogance is an admirable trait.

Be like a tree, sway and bend but never break.

✧

If someone says they have no faults
then there is probably something
seriously wrong with them.

Nomads are the most skilled at finding the best pastures, and villagers are the most skilled at pleasing the deities.

✧

Every man or woman has their own way of thinking, and every village has its own traditions and customs.

If you become wealthy through dishonesty don't expect it to last. Your bad deeds will catch up with you.

❖

If you are unhappy even a beautiful Summer's day will feel like the cold heart of winter.

A herd of goats will have trouble toppling
a strong tree, and bad people will find it
hard to bring down a good person.

✧

If farm animals have proper shelter a hawk
will not be happy in its mountain nest.

When a goat is killed the sheep shivers.

❖

A happy man in filthy rags is richer than
a miserable merchant dressed in finery.

Like high mountains seeing others
but never meeting, some kindred
spirits are destined to live apart.

❖

The higher the mountain, the deeper the abyss
The greater the gain, the more potential for loss
The deeper the dharma, the more
numerous are the obstacles.

A great mountain will not be moved by wind and a great ocean cannot be burned by fire.

❖

Like a wild animal always wanting more meat, human desire is never satisfied.

If people respect each other the
way they respect the Buddha they
will have a peaceful life.

❖

Rich and powerful people will desert you
if you lose your money and power —
there is a lesson to be learned here.

We point a spear at others even
though we cannot bear our fingers
to be pricked by a needle.

We disguise our mountains of faults but
find valleys of faults with others.

If you dispense with negativity you
are on the Buddhist path.

❖

If it does not ferment it is not beer.
If it doesn't grow and develop
it's not a true mind.

Intelligence is like fresh snow on the mountain
And stupidity is like a forest gutted by fire.

❖

Beware of speeches which have the
same three elements: 'I did not see,' 'I
did not know,' 'I was not aware.'

As a stone is wedged in place to stabilise a pillar a good mediator will sort out a dispute.

✧

If you live a long life you will experience three kinds of happiness and three kinds of suffering.

Don't let your disagreements outlive you.

✦

Even a small horse can come from good
breeding, and even if I am short I may
still be descended from Padme Lingpa*.

*The spiritual treasure revealer.

A human's happiness is in its mind,
a dog's happiness is in its tail.

✧

You get to know your horse by riding it for
a long time, as you get to know people
by spending a lot of time talking
with them and drinking tea.

If actions are not carried out with a pure
heart it is as if gold becomes sand.

✧

Even mature people need guidance,
as clever people need inspiration.

If you become poor and your relatives reject
you, you can only be enriched by leaving them.

᛭

You will only truly realize the peace and
happiness in your own country when
you travel around the world.

A man may be buried in the ground, but his words will still be carried by the winds.

A human without faults is a Buddha.
A Buddha with faults is a human.

Unpleasant medicine will sometimes cure you
in the same way that people you don't
like will sometimes benefit you.

·:·

Good people's minds are like gold,
they never change colour.

A good old dog will protect you from
fierce robbers in the same way that old
people will guard the wisdom of history.

❖

Don't stare too much with your eyes, or
blare too much with your mouth.

Even though you climb the tree of fame and success you are not immune from falling to the ground and breaking your bones.

❖

As flowers are the ornaments of the fields, the proverbs of the scholars are the ornaments of the community.

If you drink too much of anything, even
Mother's milk, you will get indigestion.
If you hear too much of anything, you
will stop listening and fall asleep.

❖

Achieving results without hardship
is like saying you will only eat fish
which does not have scales.

For some a happy life is dependent on
wealth, but the happiness of the next
life only depends on the dharma.

❖

Even the most cherished body in life
will become the food of vultures
and worms at the end.

The next life is always longer than this one,
just as the lord of death is fiercer
than any present ruler.

✵

A tailor is never satisfied with his alterations,
but he is always satisfied with
the leftover pieces of cloth.

A donkey is burdened by his heavy load as
a shopkeeper is burdened by always
wanting more customers.

❖

Traders are not always honest and thieves
rarely spend money wisely.

Wounds made by weapons can heal,
wounds made by harsh words
leave terrible emotional scars.

✦

Your beloved child can lie to you, and your
hated enemy can teach you some wisdom.

Your five fingers are like brothers and
each has its own hand of fate.

✧

This fickle human life usually ends with
one long sigh and one long night.

A bad night's sleep can make you
feel tired for ten days.

✧

Your face can have the glow of a lotus but
your mind can be as dark as an ink stain.

When you see the person you love the sight
is rapturous, and when you hear their
voice it is like listening to music,
and the devotion grows.

❖

Even if the terms of a peace treaty cannot be
agreed violent war should always be avoided.

Words that will hurt another should
be stopped, like a boulder which is
about to crash onto a building.

If you gloat at other's misfortune you may
soon be mired in your own unhappiness.

The only way to find our own
faults is to look in the mirror.

❖

A person with high standards who helps others
is like a king or queen in their own community.

Leftover food becomes food for rats,
leftover clothes becomes food for moths.

✧

When someone says, 'come eat and
drink' the ears perk up. When someone
says, 'come to work' the ears go flat.

You may enjoy food at other people's houses,
but the best bed is always in your own home.

❖

If your wealth disappears you
involuntarily become a yogi.

Some conversations are hard to start as
some tasks are difficult to conclude.

⸎

Giving to others is the gateway to compassion
but many would prefer to accumulate
possessions just for themselves.

If you take the jungle away from a
free, roaming snow leopard it will
feel like a poor street dog.

❖

The more dark clouds gather on the
mountaintop the more the water
in the river will rage below.

Tigers have eighteen ways of leaping, but jackals have nineteen ways of hiding.

❖

The misfortune of someone born in the Tiger year is transferred to someone born in the Rabbit year.

The more affluent and powerful you become
the less you should spoil your children.

⁕

Human life is as transient and impermanent
as the setting sun is on the horizon.

Look carefully, there is a big difference
between mist and smoke.

✧

If you are committed to a spiritual life this
and the next life will be happy,
if not both will be ruined.

If you are in a beautiful flower-filled meadow
you will sing with joy, if you are at the
edge of a cliff you will cry out in fear.

❖

Never leave the Lama who shows you the
path to liberation until you have
attained Buddhahood.

If striving for success fills you with fear, you are better to stay home and do meditation.

❖

If you throw dust up into the air, some will fall on others but most will fall on yourself.

An ocean is a collection of drops, a rock is a collection of particles, but they are of equal value. The same is true for the love you have in your heart and mind.

✧

Do not attempt to summit the mountain unless you are prepared to fall down the crevasse.

Virtuous deeds and dire suffering can
both lead to divine happiness.

Defeat is part of the price you
can pay for victory.

If you don't have horns you are not a bull, and if you are not warm and friendly you can't be happy.

❖

The King of Medicine is Anu, who says there are more who die than recover. The King of Poison is Tsendug who says there are more who recover than die.

Eat in accordance with the seasons as you would dress for different types of weather.

✣

Mushrooms always rise to the surface.

People worry about rich people who are sick,
but forget about poor people who are dying.

❖

The wealth of the devout goes to charity.
The wealth of the arrogant goes to the enemy.
The wealth of the miser is eaten by bugs.

Betelnut, the leaf, and the lime—
if one important ingredient is missing
the flavour is lost—just like life.

❖

In order to achieve great results you
have to let go of minor matters.

Just as the wind knows what is light
or heavy, people instinctively know
who is of higher or lower ranking.

❖

The fir tree and the bamboo are different
plant species but both grow tall and strong.

An ugly face worries the owner and an ugly thought worries your companion.

✧

The place to distinguish gold from brass is at the smithy.
The place to distinguish fact from fiction is at the courthouse.

Do not seek refuge in demons and charlatans.
Keep your faith in the protective deities.

✧

The demons are powerful but the
Buddha's truth will always prevail.

When there are no fellow archers around you
will be the one shooting the best arrows.

✧

Explain things to people who ask, and
teach to those who yearn to learn.

Don't trust a snarling wild dog, nor
trust someone you don't know.

✢

Hell is close to the grave of a sinner, and
liberation is near the place of an enlightened
one's departure to the next life.

Rather live a short happy life
than a long unhappy one.

✧

When we are ill it is medicine which
heals us. And when we are dying it is
the dharma which is our salvation.

If there were no tigers in the forest there would be no end to monkey business.

❖

If there is no harmony at home, you will not be successful in the outside world.

You can die from over-eating or hunger. As
ever the best path is always the middle way.

✧

Without inner awareness the eyes seeing
the world might as well be blind.

As a drowning man grabs at anything
to save himself, so a liar will say
anything to salvage his reputation.

⁂

Just like you would not be picky with food
if you were starving, do not be choosey
with doctors if you are seriously ill.

Be aware of the power of the gods, but don't ignore the presence of the devils.

When you have the wealth of a rat, you will also have the suffering of a rat. When you have the wealth of a horse you will also have the suffering of a horse.

When a jewel is in your hand you
don't value it.
That only happens when you lose
it to someone else.

✢

Just as anything can grow well in a Summer
meadow, anything can happen
in the yogi's experience.

The greatest wealth is generosity, and the most sublime happiness is to reach the state of bodhicitta.*

*Bodhicitta in Buddhism means being able to bring happiness to all sentient beings.

❖

If you don't cultivate a good mind it will disappear like a shooting star in the sky.

If you want to action great ideas you need to
apply the strength of a Himalayan mountain.

❖

If you are a true monk you will not be
greedy, and if you are a true yogi
you will be free of fixed ideas.

The cause of both happiness and sorrow
is the result of your previous actions.

❖

Telling other people what to do is easy,
telling yourself what to do is very difficult.

A hero in battle can overcome one, a hero in learning can conquer a generation.

✣

The children of a loving mother are as happy as the subjects of a Bodhisattva.*

*Enlightened being.

You should not bow to every ruler, or seek
empowerments from every Lama.

✧

A benevolent ruler is prized by his subjects
in the same way that a good Lama
is praised by divine beings.

Don't fear the ruler, only fear his power.

❖

If you ask a favour from a King, the decision as
to whether or not it will be granted will
most likely come from his trusted attendant.

You cannot eliminate the wrinkles on your face, nor can you erase any of your past actions.

⁘

The stillness of a lion is better than the scampering of a monkey.

The beggar endures the suffering of hunger, and the rich man endures the suffering of a hoarder.

❖

Just like pearls come from the ocean,
most reincarnated beings are born
into the families of Lamas.

A father's son is like a white snow lion, even if the child ends up behaving like a village dog.

✧

Having loving parents is no guarantee that your fate will go in a similarly positive direction.

If you abandon or are unkind to your parents you will ruin your life and the next one.

✧

Sons of the same father can have different ways of living just as those sharing a pillow will have different dreams.

Happiness as you grow up is like the phases
of the moon, it waxes and wanes.

When your parents are alive you are not
always aware of their affection, after
they die you always feel their love.

Don't take responsibility for someone who
cannot take responsibility for themselves.

✧

An authentic person will speak
when necessary.
A mediocre person will speak when questioned.
A lesser person will only speak
behind your back.

As it takes a while to break in a new horse,
so it takes a while for an inexperienced
person to learn how to tell good stories.

❖

Even if a man is not well off he must
provide, but if a woman is well
off she must still receive.

Even if a piglet could dance it would
not be considered a ballerina.

✧

If a relative doesn't help you they are a stranger.
If a stranger helps you they are like a good relative!

The rich inheritance of good parents
can be the source of gambling
money for degenerate offspring.

✵

Speak in accordance with your
audience and cook in accordance with
the ingredients in your larder.

Wars are fought and won by ordinary soldiers,
but it is the chief who receives all the adulation.

During the harvesting of sweet buckwheat
both the master and servant
should pitch in equally.

Even hawks and eagles must
sometimes touch the ground.

❖

While you are looking for a needle outside you
will be more likely to lose the axe at home.

Army chiefs almost always live
longer than their soldiers.

❖

In public a man can be the favourite of his
officer, and in private he can be the
sweetheart of the officer's wife.

Outer dirt can be removed by
washing, but inner dirt cannot always
be removed by explanation.

✦

If wealthy people do not practice generosity,
in the end they will be the caretaker
of that property for others.

Wanting more money makes the
rich more work, and wanting more
food makes the beggar work.

✦

You cannot eat tsampa* and play
the flute at the same time.

*Flour and water

Protect your possessions from a robber,
but give your things to a beggar.

✧

Better to milk the cow and drink that
milk, than kill the cow and eat its meat.

Bad children do not remember the time of their parent's death and bad parents do not remember the time of their childrens' birth.

⁂

If you have no son then get a son-in-law, and if you have no daughter then get a daughter-in-law.

Bribes and presents are tempting for some
judges in the same way that women
are tempting for some holy people.

✧

The donkey has many ways of sleeping but his
owner has many ways of making him work.

When birds get old they look for their nests.
When people get old they want to be home.

⁙

Just as the old tortoise loses the shine
on his shell so the demented person
lacks his sharpness of mind.

Until enlightenment is attained you rely on your spiritual master. When enlightenment is attained you are equal.

❖

In a house with no cats mice reign supreme.

If the Lama is allowed to kill the chicken it will encourage his attendant to steal the eggs.

✦

A student may listen to the Lama's teaching about the dharma but may still only have blind faith.

For the powerful, there is power but
little intelligence.
For the intelligent there is intelligence,
but little power.

✧

Too many chant masters will distort the ritual
as too many judges will distort the verdict.

Anything can grow in a fertile meadow, and
anything can arise in an unstable mind.

⁝

The sound of thunder is loud, but it is empty.
The rainbow has pretty colours, but
soon vanishes into emptiness.

Although the takin* dies thin, it still
weighs many yak loads. But if the rat dies
healthy it can still fit into your hand.

*Himalayan buck.

Just like the snakes coils will be released
by movement, so the knots in the mind
will be released by repentance.

A yogi should not linger at the
wealthy devotee's house.

✦

Speaking without an audience is
like an echo in an empty cave.

If an ordinary man holds his head high it
is hard for an official to put him down.

⟡

If you don't contemplate those that suffer
compassion is just an empty word.

Give someone a bedroom to sleep in and they
may wish to dwell in your other rooms.

❖

Just as you should not drink too much
tea before bedtime, do not talk
too much on your deathbed.

Looking for faults in the innocent is like looking for corners on an egg.

✧

Dreams without sleeping are like galloping without a horse.

Don't reply when you are feeling sleepy,
and don't repent when you are dying.

❖

With close family even a small meal is very
nourishing, as things once decided don't
have to be discussed in more detail.

A poor field will one day yield a bumper
crop, as a disappointing relative will
one day do the right thing by you.

❖

A group of young male deer travelling
together may have different lengths of antlers,
but they will leave the same hoofprints.

Some gains are a genuine step forward,
others are the beginning of a nightmare.

✧

If you speak your mind too openly, you
may end up covering your lips
with your hands in regret.

Sometimes the only things a poor man
has left is an empty mouth and
and an empty hand.

✧

Whenever you ride your horse be aware
that there are ants on the ground.

You cannot put two saddles on one horse, nor can there be two great masters for the one doctrine.

✧

Before mounting a saddled horse, pat the saddle three times.

Better to be thrown by a horse, than
to be thrown out by a king.

⁂

When a mare is frisky it will chase the
stallion, and when a woman wants
her husband she sings a song.

A donkey can block a horse's path, and a devil can block a Buddhist practitioner's path.

If you can't be ahead of a hundred horses, don't get behind a hundred donkeys.

Crows will pick out the eyes of a horse before it dies, just as the wealth of a person can be taken before they die.

❖

We don't have enough eyes for all that can be seen, or enough thoughts for everything which can be contemplated.

The most delicious food is inside the basket,
like the best love making is under the quilt!

⟡

Food left uneaten can be re-heated later,
but words left unsaid can leave
a sour taste in the mouth.

Big celebrations last for one day, but a family argument can last for much longer.

✧

If you are starving do not sell the family home, and if you are thirsty do not drink alcohol—just water.

Without humour poor conversation will result.
Without careful preparation your spiritual
practice will have no meaning.

❖

Churn milk a hundred times and you will
make butter, speak a mantra a hundred
times and you will distill the essence.

Timeless words of wisdom are like messages inscribed on a rock. Even if the rock breaks the wisdom remains.

✧

Totally honest house-guests are rare, just as judges rarely give completely honest verdicts.

Pots without handles are hard to hold, in the
same way that complicated metaphors
are hard to understand.

❖

Gossip passed on usually gathers momentum,
but food passed on always decreases.

Words are not weapons but they
can still shatter the heart.

Our last words are our will, and our
last clothes are our burial cloths.

Digging into the meaning of words
is like digging in mud. The deeper
you go the more you will find.

❖

Name' Same', Kadin Chhe' Chhe'

Thank you beyond the sky and the earth.

⁂